Interview Gu

For

UI/UX Designers

100 Questions and Answers

Patrick Cleftt

Unlock the secrets to acing your UI/UX design interviews with 'Interview Guide for UI/UX Designers'. Dive into this comprehensive guide packed with expert insights, strategies, and real-world scenarios to help you navigate the complexities of the design interview process with confidence and poise. Whether you're a seasoned professional or just starting your career in UI/UX design, this book equips you with the tools and knowledge to showcase your skills and land your dream job. Get ready to impress interviewers and secure your place in the competitive world of design.

1. **Question: What is the difference between UI and UX design?**

   Answer: UI (User Interface) design focuses on the look and feel of a product, including its visual elements like colours, typography, and layout, as well as its interactive components such as buttons and navigation menus. UX (User Experience) design, on the other hand, encompasses the entire journey a user takes with a product, from their first interaction to their last. It involves understanding user needs, conducting research, creating wireframes and prototypes, and testing the product to ensure it is intuitive, efficient, and delightful to use. While UI design deals with the surface-level aesthetics, UX design is concerned with the overall usability and satisfaction of the user experience.

2. **Question: Can you explain the importance of user research in the design process?**

   Answer: User research is essential in the design process as it provides valuable insights into the behaviours, preferences, and pain points of the target audience. By conducting user research, designers can gain a deep understanding of their users' needs and motivations, which allows them to create products that are tailored to their specific requirements. User research methods such as interviews, surveys, and usability testing help designers uncover valuable insights that inform design decisions, leading to more user-centric and effective solutions. Ultimately, user research ensures that designers create products that meet the needs of their users and deliver a positive user experience.

3. **Question: How do you approach creating user personas?**

   Answer: Creating user personas involves researching and synthesizing data about the target audience to create fictional representations of typical users. To create user personas, I start by conducting user interviews, surveys, and market research to gather information about the target audience's demographics, behaviours, goals, and pain points. I then analyse this data to identify common patterns and trends, which I use to create detailed personas that represent different user segments. Each persona includes information such as age, gender, occupation, goals, challenges, and preferences, as well as a fictional name and photo to humanize the persona. These personas serve as a reference point throughout the design process, helping me empathize with users and make informed design decisions that prioritize their needs and preferences.

4. **Question: What tools do you use for wireframing and prototyping?**

   Answer: For wireframing, I typically use tools like Sketch, Adobe XD, or Figma, which allow me to create low-fidelity representations of the user interface. These tools provide a quick and easy way to sketch out ideas and iterate on designs without getting bogged down by details. When it comes to prototyping, I prefer using tools like InVision or Axure, which allow me to create interactive prototypes that simulate the user interaction with the product. These prototyping tools enable me to create clickable prototypes that can be shared with stakeholders and tested with users to gather feedback and validate design decisions. Additionally, I also use tools like Marvel or Proto.io for more advanced prototyping capabilities, such as animations and micro-interactions, to create highly interactive and engaging prototypes.

5. **Question: How do you ensure accessibility in your designs?**

   Answer: Accessibility is a critical aspect of design that ensures products can be used by people of all abilities, including those with disabilities. To ensure accessibility in my designs, I follow best practices such as adhering to WCAG (Web Content Accessibility Guidelines) standards, which provide guidelines for creating accessible web content. This includes considerations such as providing alternative text for images, ensuring sufficient colour contrast for readability, and designing keyboard-friendly interfaces. Additionally, I conduct accessibility audits and usability testing with users who have disabilities to identify and address any accessibility issues in my designs. By prioritizing accessibility, I ensure that my designs are inclusive and can be used by everyone, regardless of their abilities.

6. **Question: What methods do you use to gather user feedback?**

   Answer: Gathering user feedback is essential for validating design decisions and ensuring that the product meets the needs of its users. To gather user feedback, I use a variety of methods, including interviews, surveys, usability testing, and analytics. Interviews allow me to have in-depth conversations with users to understand their needs, preferences, and pain points. Surveys help me gather feedback from a larger audience and quantify user opinions and preferences. Usability testing involves observing users as they interact with prototypes or existing products to identify usability issues and gather insights for improvement. Analytics provide quantitative data about user behaviour, such as page views, click-through rates, and conversion rates, which I use to track the performance of the product and identify areas for optimization. By using a combination of these methods, I gather comprehensive feedback from users that informs design decisions and helps improve the overall user experience.

7. **Question: Describe your approach to creating a seamless user flow.**

   Answer: Creating a seamless user flow involves mapping out the steps a user takes to accomplish a task within a product and designing intuitive pathways that guide users through the process effortlessly. My approach to creating a seamless user flow starts with understanding the user's goals and objectives and identifying the key tasks they need to complete. I then create a flowchart or user journey map that outlines the steps involved in achieving those tasks, taking into account various user touchpoints and interactions. During this process, I prioritize simplicity and clarity, minimizing the number of steps and reducing cognitive load for users. I also ensure consistency in design elements and navigation patterns to provide a cohesive and familiar experience across the product. Once the user flow is mapped out, I create wireframes or prototypes to visualize the flow and test it with users to gather feedback and iterate on the design. Through iteration and testing, I refine the user flow to address any pain points or usability issues and create a seamless and intuitive experience for users.

8. **Question: How do you ensure consistency and coherence in your designs across different screens and pages?**

   Answer: Consistency and coherence are essential principles in design that help users navigate and understand a product more easily. To ensure consistency and coherence in my designs, I establish a set of design principles and guidelines that govern the use of colours, typography, spacing, and other visual elements. I create a design system or style guide that documents these principles and provides reusable components and patterns for consistency across different screens and pages. This design system serves as a reference for me and other team members, ensuring that everyone follows the same design standards and maintains consistency throughout the product. Additionally, I conduct regular design reviews and audits to identify any inconsistencies or deviations from the established guidelines and make adjustments as needed to maintain coherence and alignment with the overall design vision.

9. **Question: What are some strategies you use to create intuitive and user-friendly navigation?**

   Answer: Intuitive and user-friendly navigation is essential for helping users find what they're looking for quickly and easily. To create intuitive navigation, I follow several strategies: First, I prioritize simplicity and clarity, minimizing the number of navigation options and using clear labels and icons that are easy to understand. Second, I organize content logically and hierarchically, grouping related items together and providing multiple pathways for users to navigate through the product. Third, I use familiar navigation patterns and conventions that users are already familiar with, such as top or side navigation bars, breadcrumbs, and search bars. Fourth, I provide feedback and visual cues to indicate the user's current location and progress within the product, such as highlighting active navigation items or providing breadcrumbs. Finally, I conduct usability testing with real users to gather feedback on the navigation and identify any pain points or areas for improvement, iteratively refining the navigation to create a seamless and intuitive experience.

10. **Question: How do you incorporate user feedback into your UI/UX design iterations?**

    Answer: Incorporating user feedback into UI/UX design iterations is essential for creating user-centred solutions that meet the needs and expectations of the target audience. To incorporate user feedback, I follow a structured process: First, I collect feedback from various sources, such as user interviews, surveys, usability testing, and analytics. I then analyse this feedback to identify common themes, patterns, and pain points that inform design decisions. Based on this analysis, I prioritize the feedback and determine which changes are most critical for improving the user experience. I then iterate on the design, making adjustments and refinements based on the feedback received. Throughout this process, I involve stakeholders and other team members to ensure alignment and buy-in for the proposed changes. Finally, I test the updated design with users to validate the changes and gather additional feedback for further iteration. By incorporating user feedback into each design iteration, I ensure that the product evolves in response to user needs and preferences, ultimately leading to a more successful and user-centred solution.

11. **Question: How do you approach designing for mobile devices, considering the differences in screen sizes and user interactions?**

Answer: Designing for mobile devices requires a mobile-first approach, where I prioritize designing for smaller screens and touch interactions. I start by understanding the limitations and capabilities of different devices and screen sizes, considering factors such as screen resolution, aspect ratio, and pixel density. I then create responsive designs that adapt to various screen sizes and orientations, ensuring that the user experience remains consistent across devices. Additionally, I optimize interactions for touch input, such as using larger tap targets and designing intuitive swipe gestures, to accommodate the mobile user's behaviour.

12. **Question: Can you explain the importance of usability testing in the design process, and how do you conduct usability tests?**

Answer: Usability testing is crucial for evaluating the effectiveness and usability of a design from the user's perspective. It helps identify usability issues, gather feedback, and validate design decisions. To conduct usability tests, I recruit representative users who match the target audience demographics and create realistic tasks for them to perform. I then observe and record their interactions with the design, noting any difficulties, errors, or areas of confusion. After the test, I analyse the results, identify patterns and insights, and use them to iteratively improve the design.

13. **Question: What are some common usability heuristics, and how do you apply them in your designs?**

Answer: Usability heuristics are a set of general principles that guide the evaluation of user interfaces. Some common usability heuristics include visibility of system status, match between system and the real world, and user control and freedom. In my designs, I apply these heuristics by ensuring clear and consistent feedback to users about the system's status, using familiar language and metaphors that align with the user's mental model, and providing users with control and flexibility to navigate and interact with the interface.

14. **Question: How do you prioritize features and functionalities in your designs, considering business goals and user needs?**

    Answer: Prioritizing features and functionalities involves balancing business objectives with user needs and preferences. I start by conducting user research to understand the target audience and their goals, pain points, and preferences. I then prioritize features based on their impact on the user experience, business value, and technical feasibility. I use techniques such as MoSCoW prioritization (Must have, Should have, Could have, Won't have) or the Kano model to categorize features according to their importance and urgency. By prioritizing features in this way, I ensure that the design addresses the most critical user needs and aligns with the business objectives.

15. **Question: How do you ensure consistency in your UI designs across different platforms, such as web and mobile?**

    Answer: Ensuring consistency in UI designs across different platforms involves creating a unified design system that governs the use of visual elements, interaction patterns, and branding guidelines. I start by defining a set of design principles and standards that apply across all platforms, such as colour palette, typography, and spacing. I then create reusable components and patterns, such as buttons, cards, and navigation bars, that can be used consistently across different platforms. Additionally, I maintain a centralized design system or style guide that serves as a single source of truth for design assets and guidelines, ensuring consistency and coherence in the UI designs across all platforms.

16. **Question: How do you approach creating accessible designs that are inclusive of users with disabilities?**

Answer: Creating accessible designs involves considering the needs of users with disabilities and ensuring that the design is usable by everyone, regardless of their abilities. I start by familiarizing myself with accessibility guidelines, such as the Web Content Accessibility Guidelines (WCAG), and incorporating them into my design process. This includes considerations such as providing alternative text for images, ensuring sufficient color contrast for readability, and designing keyboard-friendly interfaces. I also conduct accessibility audits and usability testing with users who have disabilities to identify and address any accessibility barriers in the design. By prioritizing accessibility in my designs, I ensure that they are inclusive and can be used by everyone, regardless of their abilities.

17. **Question: Describe your approach to creating a user-centred design.**

Answer: Creating a user-centred design involves understanding the needs, behaviours, and preferences of the target audience and designing solutions that meet their needs effectively. My approach starts with conducting user research to gather insights into the target audience's demographics, goals, pain points, and preferences. I then use these insights to create user personas and user journeys that represent different user segments and their interactions with the product. Throughout the design process, I prioritize user feedback and iterate on designs based on user testing and validation. By involving users in every stage of the design process, I ensure that the final product is tailored to their needs and delivers a positive user experience.

18. **Question: How do you balance creativity and usability in your designs?**

Answer: Balancing creativity and usability involves finding a harmonious blend between innovative design solutions and practical considerations for usability. I start by exploring creative ideas and pushing the boundaries of design while keeping the user's needs and preferences in mind. I then evaluate these ideas against usability principles and best practices to ensure that they are intuitive, efficient, and easy to use. Throughout the design process, I iterate on designs based on user feedback and usability testing, refining the balance between creativity and usability to create solutions that are both visually appealing and functional.

19. **Question: How do you incorporate brand identity and guidelines into your UI designs?**

    Answer: Incorporating brand identity and guidelines into UI designs involves aligning the visual elements and aesthetics of the design with the brand's personality, values, and visual language. I start by familiarizing myself with the brand's identity guidelines, including its logo, color palette, typography, and imagery style. I then incorporate these elements into the UI designs, ensuring that they reflect the brand's personality and create a consistent brand experience. Additionally, I adhere to brand guidelines for consistency in layout, spacing, and proportions, maintaining a cohesive visual language across all touchpoints. By prioritizing brand consistency and integrity, I strengthen brand recognition and loyalty among users.

20. **Question: How do you approach designing for internationalization and localization?**

    Answer: Designing for internationalization and localization involves creating designs that can be easily adapted to different languages, cultures, and regions. I start by designing with scalability and flexibility in mind, using techniques such as designing for text expansion and contraction, separating content from presentation, and using culturally neutral visuals. I also collaborate with localization teams to ensure that designs are culturally appropriate and can be easily translated into different languages. Additionally, I conduct usability testing with users from different regions to identify any cultural or linguistic barriers in the design and make adjustments as needed to improve the international user experience.

21. **Question: How do you stay updated on the latest UI/UX design trends and technologies?**

    Answer: Staying updated on the latest UI/UX design trends and technologies is essential for keeping my skills and knowledge relevant in the fast-paced field of design. I stay informed by regularly reading design blogs, articles, and publications, following industry influencers and thought leaders on social media, and attending design conferences, workshops, and webinars. I also participate in online communities and forums where designers share insights, tips, and best practices.

Additionally, I experiment with new tools and technologies, such as prototyping tools, design systems, and emerging design trends, to stay ahead of the curve and incorporate innovative solutions into my designs.

22. **Question: Describe your experience working in Agile or other iterative development methodologies.**

Answer: Working in Agile or other iterative development methodologies involves collaborating closely with cross-functional teams to deliver value to users in incremental iterations. In my experience, I have worked in Agile environments where I participated in sprint planning, daily stand-ups, and sprint reviews. I collaborated closely with product managers, developers, and other stakeholders to define user stories, prioritize features, and deliver high-quality designs on time and within budget. I embraced the iterative nature of Agile development, adapting to changes and feedback quickly and continuously improving the product based on user needs and market dynamics. Overall, my experience in Agile environments has taught me the importance of collaboration, flexibility, and responsiveness in delivering successful UI/UX designs.

23. **Question: Can you describe a time when you had to pivot your design approach based on user feedback or stakeholder input?**

Answer: Yes, there was a project where we initially designed a complex navigation structure for a mobile app, assuming that users would appreciate having access to a wide range of features and functionalities. However, during usability testing, we observed that users found the navigation confusing and overwhelming, leading to frustration and abandonment of the app. Based on this feedback, we realized the need to simplify the navigation and streamline the user flow to make it more intuitive and user-friendly. We pivoted our design approach by conducting additional user research to understand the most critical user tasks and prioritizing simplicity and clarity in the navigation. As a result, we redesigned the navigation structure, reducing the number of options and grouping related features together. We then tested the updated design with users to validate the changes, and the feedback was overwhelmingly positive, with users finding the new navigation much easier to use and navigate.

24. **Question: How do you approach designing for user retention and engagement?**

Answer: Designing for user retention and engagement involves creating experiences that are not only usable but also enjoyable and compelling, encouraging users to return to the product and engage with it regularly. To achieve this, I focus on understanding user motivations, behaviours, and triggers that drive engagement. I design features and interactions that provide value to users and make the product indispensable in their daily lives. This may include incorporating gamification elements, such as badges or rewards, to incentivize user participation, or designing personalized experiences that cater to individual user preferences and interests. I also leverage user data and analytics to track user behaviour and identify opportunities for improvement, iterating on designs based on user feedback and performance metrics to enhance user retention and engagement over time.

25. **Question: How do you approach designing for complex workflows or user tasks?**

Answer: Designing for complex workflows or user tasks requires a systematic approach that breaks down the process into manageable steps and prioritizes clarity, efficiency, and user empowerment. I start by conducting user research to understand the steps involved in the workflow and the challenges users face in completing the task. I then map out the user journey and identify key touchpoints where users interact with the product. Using this information, I design clear and intuitive interfaces that guide users through each step of the process, providing contextual cues, feedback, and assistance as needed. I also prioritize simplicity and consistency in the design, minimizing cognitive load and reducing the risk of errors or confusion. Throughout the design process, I iterate on designs based on user feedback and usability testing, refining the workflow to optimize usability and user satisfaction.

26. **Question: How do you ensure that your designs are scalable and maintainable as the product evolves?**

Answer: Ensuring that designs are scalable and maintainable involves adopting a modular and systematic approach that allows for flexibility and adaptability as the product evolves. I start by creating a design system or style guide that documents the design principles, patterns, and components used throughout the product. This design system serves as a centralized repository of reusable assets and guidelines, ensuring consistency and coherence across all screens and pages. I also collaborate closely with developers to ensure that designs are implemented accurately and efficiently, using techniques such as atomic design or component-based design to create scalable and modular UI elements. Additionally, I conduct regular design reviews and audits to identify any inconsistencies or deviations from the design system and make adjustments as needed to maintain scalability and maintainability over time.

27. **Question: How do you approach designing for emotional engagement and brand affinity?**

Answer: Designing for emotional engagement and brand affinity involves creating experiences that resonate with users on an emotional level and foster a strong connection with the brand. To achieve this, I focus on understanding the emotional drivers and aspirations of the target audience, as well as the brand's personality, values, and visual identity. I design experiences that evoke positive emotions, such as joy, excitement, or trust, through thoughtful use of color, imagery, and storytelling. I also leverage emotional design principles, such as delight, surprise, and anticipation, to create memorable moments that leave a lasting impression on users. Additionally, I ensure that the design reflects the brand's personality and values, using consistent branding elements and messaging to reinforce brand identity and build affinity with users. By prioritizing emotional engagement in my designs, I create experiences that not only meet user needs but also inspire loyalty and advocacy for the brand.

28. **Question: How do you approach designing for cross-platform consistency, such as web and mobile?**

Answer: Designing for cross-platform consistency involves creating a unified and cohesive experience that translates seamlessly across different devices and screen sizes. To achieve this, I start by establishing a set of design principles and guidelines that apply across all platforms, such as color palette, typography, and spacing. I then create responsive designs that adapt to various screen sizes and orientations, ensuring that the user experience remains consistent regardless of the device. Additionally, I use platform-specific design patterns and conventions to optimize the experience for each platform, taking into account factors such as input methods, screen resolutions, and interaction paradigms. Throughout the design process, I maintain a centralized design system or style guide that serves as a single source of truth for design assets and guidelines, ensuring consistency and coherence across all touchpoints.

29. **Question: Can you describe a time when you had to balance conflicting requirements or priorities in a design project?**

Answer: Yes, there was a project where we had conflicting requirements from different stakeholders regarding the prioritization of features and functionalities. Some stakeholders prioritized adding new features to enhance the product's capabilities, while others prioritized improving performance and stability to address existing issues. To balance these conflicting requirements, I facilitated discussions and workshops with stakeholders to align on the project goals and priorities. We conducted user research and usability testing to gather data and insights that informed our decision-making process. We then prioritized features and functionalities based on their impact on user experience, business value, and technical feasibility, finding a compromise that addressed the needs of all stakeholders while maintaining a focus on delivering value to users. By fostering open communication and collaboration among stakeholders, we were able to overcome the conflicting requirements and deliver a successful design solution that met the needs of the project.

30. **Question: How do you approach designing for conversion optimization and user engagement metrics?**

Answer: Designing for conversion optimization and user engagement involves creating experiences that drive desired actions and behaviours from users, such as sign-ups, purchases, or referrals. To achieve this, I start by defining clear conversion goals and key performance indicators (KPIs) that align with the business objectives. I then conduct user research and usability testing to understand the factors that influence user behaviour and identify opportunities for improvement. Using insights from this research, I design intuitive and persuasive user interfaces that guide users towards the desired actions, using techniques such as clear calls-to-action, social proof, and urgency messaging. I also leverage A/B testing and multivariate testing to experiment with different design variations and measure their impact on conversion rates and user engagement metrics. By continuously optimizing designs based on data-driven insights, I improve conversion rates and user engagement, ultimately driving business growth and success.

31. **Question: How do you approach designing for diverse user personas with different needs and preferences?**

   Answer: Designing for diverse user personas involves understanding the unique needs, preferences, and behaviours of different user segments and creating solutions that accommodate their varying requirements. To achieve this, I start by creating detailed user personas that represent different demographic groups, such as age, gender, occupation, and geographic location, as well as psychographic factors, such as goals, motivations, and pain points. I then conduct user research and usability testing with representatives from each persona group to gather insights and validate design decisions. Using this information, I design flexible and adaptable solutions that cater to the needs of diverse user personas, such as customizable settings, personalized recommendations, or alternative pathways for completing tasks. By prioritizing inclusivity and diversity in my designs, I ensure that the product is accessible and usable by users from all backgrounds and walks of life.

32. **Question: How do you approach designing for complex data visualization and information architecture?**

   Answer: Designing for complex data visualization and information architecture involves organizing and presenting large amounts of data in a clear, understandable, and visually engaging manner. To achieve this, I start by understanding the structure and hierarchy of the data and identifying the key insights and relationships that need to be communicated to users. I then create wireframes and prototypes to explore different layout and visualization options, using techniques such as hierarchical navigation, interactive filters, and data-driven visualizations to enhance comprehension and exploration. Throughout the design process, I prioritize simplicity and clarity, minimizing clutter and cognitive load for users while maximizing the effectiveness of the data presentation. I also conduct usability testing with representative users to gather feedback and validate design decisions, iteratively refining the data visualization and information architecture to optimize usability and user experience.

33. **Question: How do you approach designing for emerging technologies, such as augmented reality (AR) or virtual reality (VR)?**

Answer: Designing for emerging technologies such as augmented reality (AR) or virtual reality (VR) involves exploring new interaction paradigms and design principles that leverage the unique capabilities of these technologies. To achieve this, I start by researching and understanding the capabilities and constraints of the technology, as well as the user behaviours and preferences associated with it. I then collaborate with cross-functional teams, including developers, engineers, and content creators, to brainstorm and prototype innovative experiences that push the boundaries of traditional UI/UX design. Throughout the design process, I prioritize user testing and feedback to validate the effectiveness and usability of the designs, iterating on them based on insights and observations. By embracing emerging technologies and pushing the boundaries of design innovation, I create immersive and engaging experiences that captivate users and deliver value in new and exciting ways.

34. **Question: Can you describe a time when you had to advocate for user-centred design principles within your organization?**

Answer: Yes, there was a project where stakeholders were pushing for a feature-heavy design that prioritized adding new functionalities over addressing usability issues and user feedback. As the UI/UX designer on the project, I felt strongly about advocating for user-centred design principles to ensure that the product met the needs and expectations of its users. To advocate for user-centred design, I gathered data and insights from user research, usability testing, and analytics to demonstrate the importance of addressing user needs and pain points. I presented this information to stakeholders in meetings and workshops, highlighting the potential risks and consequences of neglecting user-centred design principles, such as decreased user satisfaction, increased churn, and negative brand perception. I also proposed alternative design solutions that prioritized simplicity, clarity, and usability, aligning with the needs and preferences of the target audience. By advocating for user-centred design principles and providing evidence-based recommendations, I was able to influence stakeholders and gain buy-in for a more user-centric approach to the design, ultimately leading to a more successful and impactful product.

35. **Question: How do you approach designing for accessibility in your UI/UX designs?**

    Answer: Designing for accessibility involves creating experiences that are inclusive and usable by people of all abilities, including those with disabilities. To achieve this, I start by familiarizing myself with accessibility guidelines, such as the Web Content Accessibility Guidelines (WCAG), and incorporating them into my design process. This includes considerations such as providing alternative text for images, ensuring sufficient colour contrast for readability, and designing keyboard-friendly interfaces. I also conduct accessibility audits and usability testing with users who have disabilities to identify and address any accessibility barriers in the design. By prioritizing accessibility in my designs, I ensure that they are inclusive and can be used by everyone, regardless of their abilities.

36. **Question: How do you ensure that your designs are user-friendly for older adults or users with limited technology literacy?**

    Answer: Designing for older adults or users with limited technology literacy involves simplifying the user interface and interactions to accommodate their needs and preferences. To achieve this, I prioritize clarity, simplicity, and intuitive design principles in my designs, using familiar language, icons, and metaphors that are easy to understand. I also incorporate features such as larger text sizes, clear navigation paths, and prominent call-to-action buttons to enhance usability and accessibility. Additionally, I conduct usability testing with representative users to gather feedback and identify any usability issues or areas for improvement. By prioritizing user-friendly design principles and iterating based on user feedback, I ensure that my designs are accessible and usable by users of all ages and technology literacy levels.

37. **Question: How do you approach designing for privacy and data security in your UI/UX designs?**

38. **Answer:** Designing for privacy and data security involves ensuring that users' personal information is protected and handled responsibly throughout the user journey. To achieve this, I start by conducting a privacy impact assessment to identify potential privacy risks and compliance requirements associated with the product. I then design user interfaces that provide transparency and control over the collection, use, and sharing of personal data, such as clear privacy policies, consent mechanisms, and privacy settings. Additionally, I incorporate security best practices, such as encryption, authentication, and access controls, to safeguard sensitive data from unauthorized access or breaches. Throughout the design process, I collaborate with privacy and security experts to ensure that the design meets industry standards and regulatory requirements for privacy and data protection.

39. **Question: How do you approach designing for inclusivity and diversity in your UI/UX designs?**

    Answer: Designing for inclusivity and diversity involves creating experiences that are accessible and inclusive for users from diverse backgrounds, abilities, and perspectives. To achieve this, I start by considering the needs and preferences of different user groups, including those with disabilities, language barriers, or cultural differences. I design interfaces that are flexible and adaptable, providing options for customization and personalization to accommodate diverse user needs. Additionally, I incorporate inclusive design principles, such as providing multiple pathways for completing tasks, designing for text alternatives, and avoiding stereotypes or biases in imagery and language. I also conduct usability testing with representative users to gather feedback and identify any accessibility barriers or usability issues. By prioritizing inclusivity and diversity in my designs, I ensure that the product is usable and enjoyable for users from all backgrounds and walks of life.

40. **Question: How do you approach designing for trust and credibility in your UI/UX designs?**

    Answer: Designing for trust and credibility involves creating experiences that inspire confidence and build trust among users, fostering a positive relationship between the user and the product or brand. To achieve this,

I focus on transparency, consistency, and reliability in my designs, providing clear and accurate information that users can trust. I use visual cues and branding elements to convey professionalism and authenticity, such as high-quality imagery, consistent typography, and recognizable logos. Additionally, I prioritize usability and security, designing interfaces that are easy to use and protect users' sensitive information from unauthorized access or breaches. By prioritizing trust and credibility in my designs, I create experiences that instil confidence and loyalty among users, ultimately driving engagement and success for the product or brand.

41. **Question: How do you approach designing for emotional engagement and user delight in your UI/UX designs?**

Answer: Designing for emotional engagement and user delight involves creating experiences that evoke positive emotions and create memorable moments for users. To achieve this, I focus on delighting users through thoughtful interactions, animations, and micro-interactions that surprise and delight them. I use techniques such as playful animations, unexpected transitions, and personalized experiences to create moments of joy and delight throughout the user journey. Additionally, I prioritize empathy and human-centred design principles, designing interfaces that resonate with users on an emotional level and make them feel understood and valued. By prioritizing emotional engagement and user delight in my designs, I create experiences that go beyond functionality to create meaningful connections with users, fostering loyalty and advocacy for the product or brand.

42. **Question: How do you approach designing for multi-channel experiences, such as web, mobile apps, and wearable devices?**

Answer: Designing for multi-channel experiences involves creating consistent and cohesive experiences across different devices and touchpoints. I start by understanding the user journey and identifying the key interactions and tasks that occur across various channels. I then create responsive designs that adapt to different screen sizes and input methods, ensuring a seamless experience for users as they transition between devices. Additionally, I leverage platform-specific design patterns and conventions to optimize the experience for each channel, taking into account factors such as screen resolutions, input methods, and interaction paradigms. By prioritizing consistency and coherence in my designs, I ensure that users can access and interact with the product seamlessly across all channels.

43. **Question: Can you describe your process for creating wireframes and prototypes?**

Answer: My process for creating wireframes and prototypes involves several stages: First, I start by defining the scope and objectives of the project, as well as the target audience and key user tasks. I then conduct user research and gather insights into user needs, behaviours, and preferences. Based on this research, I create low-fidelity wireframes to outline the basic layout and structure of the interface, focusing on content hierarchy and navigation. I then iterate on the wireframes based on feedback and validation from stakeholders and users. Once the wireframes are finalized, I create high-fidelity prototypes using tools such as Sketch, Adobe XD, or Figma, adding visual elements, interactions, and animations to simulate the user experience. I conduct usability testing with the prototypes to gather feedback and iterate on the designs, refining them until they meet the project requirements and user expectations.

44. **Question: How do you approach designing for complex user interactions, such as drag-and-drop or gestures?**

Answer: Designing for complex user interactions involves understanding the user's mental model and designing intuitive and responsive interfaces that accommodate their expectations and behaviours. To achieve this, I start by conducting user research to understand how users expect to interact with the interface and what gestures or interactions feel natural to them. I then design clear and visual affordances that indicate the available actions and guide users through the interaction process. Additionally, I leverage animation and feedback to provide real-time feedback and reinforce the connection between user actions and system responses. Throughout the design process, I conduct usability testing with representative users to validate the effectiveness and usability of the interactions, iterating on the designs based on feedback and observations.

45. **Question: How do you approach designing for content-heavy interfaces, such as news websites or e-commerce platforms?**

Answer: Designing for content-heavy interfaces involves organizing and presenting large amounts of information in a clear, understandable, and engaging manner. To achieve this, I start by conducting content audits to assess the volume and type of content available and prioritize the most relevant and valuable content for users. I then create a hierarchical information architecture that organizes the content into categories, topics, and subtopics, making it easy for users to find and navigate. Additionally, I design layouts that balance visual hierarchy, whitespace, and typography to emphasize important content and guide users' attention. I also leverage techniques such as infinite scrolling, lazy loading, and faceted search to enhance content discoverability and exploration. By prioritizing clarity, simplicity, and usability in my designs, I create content-heavy interfaces that are engaging and intuitive to use.

46. **Question: How do you approach designing for cross-cultural usability and internationalization?**

Answer: Designing for cross-cultural usability and internationalization involves creating experiences that are inclusive and accessible to users from different cultural backgrounds, languages, and regions. To achieve this, I start by conducting cultural research to understand cultural norms, preferences, and taboos that may influence user behaviour and expectations. I then design interfaces that are flexible and adaptable, providing options for customization and personalization to accommodate diverse cultural preferences. Additionally, I collaborate with localization experts to translate and adapt content for different languages and regions, ensuring that the design is culturally appropriate and resonates with the target audience. Throughout the design process, I conduct usability testing with representative users from different cultural backgrounds to gather feedback and identify any cultural or linguistic barriers in the design, iterating on the designs based on insights and observations.

47. **Question: How do you approach designing for emotion-driven experiences, such as gaming or entertainment apps?**

Answer: Designing for emotion-driven experiences involves creating immersive and engaging experiences that evoke specific emotions and responses from users. To achieve this, I start by understanding the emotional context and motivations of the target audience, as well as the desired emotional outcome of the experience. I then design interfaces that leverage storytelling, visual aesthetics, and interactive elements to evoke the desired emotions and create memorable moments for users. Additionally, I prioritize usability and accessibility, ensuring that the design is intuitive and easy to navigate, even in emotionally charged situations. Throughout the design process, I conduct usability testing and user research to gather feedback and validate the effectiveness of the emotional design elements, iterating on the designs based on insights and observations.

48. **Question: How do you approach designing for emerging technologies, such as voice interfaces or chatbots?**

Answer: Designing for emerging technologies such as voice interfaces or chatbots involves understanding the unique capabilities and constraints of these technologies and designing experiences that leverage their strengths effectively. To achieve this, I start by conducting research to understand user expectations and behaviours when interacting with voice interfaces or chatbots. I then design conversational flows and interactions that are natural and intuitive, taking into account factors such as language, tone, and context. Additionally, I leverage techniques such as persona-driven design to create relatable and engaging conversational experiences that resonate with users. Throughout the design process, I conduct usability testing and iterate on the designs based on feedback and observations, refining the conversational experience to optimize usability and user satisfaction.

49. **Question: How do you approach designing for accessibility in mobile app interfaces?**

Answer: Designing for accessibility in mobile app interfaces involves creating experiences that are inclusive and usable by people of all abilities, including those with disabilities. To achieve this, I start by familiarizing myself with accessibility guidelines, such as the Web Content Accessibility Guidelines (WCAG) and the Mobile Web Best Practices, and incorporating them into my design process. This includes considerations such as providing alternative text for images, ensuring sufficient colour contrast for readability, and designing keyboard-friendly interfaces. I also conduct accessibility audits and usability testing with users who have disabilities to identify and address any accessibility barriers in the design. By prioritizing accessibility in my mobile app interfaces, I ensure that they are accessible and usable by everyone, regardless of their abilities.

50. **Question: Can you describe your experience with user-centred design methodologies, such as Design Thinking or Lean UX?**

Answer: My experience with user-centred design methodologies includes working with cross-functional teams to apply principles and practices from methodologies such as Design Thinking and Lean UX. In my previous projects, I facilitated design workshops and brainstorming sessions to generate innovative ideas and solutions that prioritize user needs and preferences. I conducted user research and usability testing to gather insights and validate design decisions, iterating on the designs based on feedback and observations. I also collaborated closely with stakeholders and developers to ensure alignment and buy-in for the proposed solutions, using techniques such as rapid prototyping and user story mapping to visualize and communicate design concepts. By embracing user-centred design methodologies, I fostered a collaborative and iterative approach to designing solutions that deliver value to users and achieve business goals.

51. **Question: How do you approach designing for user onboarding and first-time user experiences?**

Answer: Designing for user onboarding and first-time user experiences involves creating experiences that guide users through the initial setup process and help them understand the value proposition of the product. To achieve this, I start by identifying the key actions and milestones that users need to complete to get started with the product. I then design a streamlined and intuitive onboarding flow that guides users through these actions, providing clear instructions and feedback along the way. Additionally, I leverage techniques such as progressive disclosure and contextual guidance to introduce features and functionalities gradually, minimizing cognitive overload for users. Throughout the design process, I conduct usability testing with first-time users to gather feedback and identify any usability issues or points of confusion, iterating on the onboarding experience based on insights and observations.

52. **Question: How do you approach designing for user engagement and retention in mobile app interfaces?**

   Answer: Designing for user engagement and retention in mobile app interfaces involves creating experiences that keep users coming back to the app and encourage them to stay engaged over time. To achieve this, I focus on understanding user motivations and behaviours, as well as the factors that drive long-term engagement. I design features and interactions that provide value to users and make the app indispensable in their daily lives. This may include incorporating gamification elements, such as rewards or challenges, to incentivize user participation, or designing personalized experiences that cater to individual user preferences and interests. Additionally, I leverage user data and analytics to track user behaviour and identify opportunities for improvement, iterating on designs based on user feedback and performance metrics to enhance user engagement and retention over time.

53. **Question: Can you describe your experience with usability testing and user research methodologies?**

   Answer: My experience with usability testing and user research methodologies includes conducting a variety of research activities to gather insights and validate design decisions. I have conducted user interviews, surveys, and contextual inquiries to understand user needs, preferences, and pain points. I have also facilitated usability testing sessions, both moderated and unmoderated, to evaluate prototypes and existing designs and gather feedback from users. Additionally, I have used techniques such as card sorting and journey mapping to visualize and analyse user journeys and information architecture. Through these research activities, I have gained valuable insights into user behaviour and preferences, which have informed my design decisions and led to more user-centred and effective solutions.

54. **Question: How do you approach designing for accessibility in web interfaces?**

Answer: Designing for accessibility in web interfaces involves creating experiences that are inclusive and usable by people of all abilities, including those with disabilities. To achieve this, I start by familiarizing myself with accessibility guidelines, such as the Web Content Accessibility Guidelines (WCAG), and incorporating them into my design process. This includes considerations such as providing alternative text for images, ensuring sufficient colour contrast for readability, and designing keyboard-friendly interfaces. I also conduct accessibility audits and usability testing with users who have disabilities to identify and address any accessibility barriers in the design. By prioritizing accessibility in my web interfaces, I ensure that they are accessible and usable by everyone, regardless of their abilities.

55. **Question: Can you describe a time when you had to design for a highly regulated industry, such as healthcare or finance?**

Answer: Yes, there was a project where I had to design a mobile app for a healthcare organization that required compliance with strict regulatory requirements, such as HIPAA (Health Insurance Portability and Accountability Act). To ensure compliance, I collaborated closely with legal and compliance experts to understand the regulatory requirements and incorporate them into the design process. This included implementing robust security measures to protect patient data, such as encryption and access controls, as well as ensuring clear and transparent privacy policies and consent mechanisms. Additionally, I conducted usability testing with healthcare professionals and patients to gather feedback and identify any usability issues or concerns related to compliance. By prioritizing compliance and user-centred design principles, I was able to deliver a successful and compliant design solution that met the needs of the organization and its users.

56. **Question: How do you approach designing for personalization and customization in user interfaces?**

Answer: Designing for personalization and customization involves creating experiences that adapt to individual user preferences and behaviours, providing tailored and relevant content and interactions. To achieve this, I start by collecting user data and preferences through user registration, user activity tracking, and user feedback mechanisms. I then use this data to create user profiles and segmentation criteria that categorize users based on their demographics, behaviour, and preferences. Using these user profiles, I design interfaces that dynamically adjust content, layout, and interactions based on the user's profile and context. This may include personalized recommendations, customized user interfaces, or adaptive user experiences that evolve over time based on user interactions and feedback. By prioritizing personalization and customization in my designs, I create experiences that are more engaging, relevant, and satisfying for users.

57. **Question: How do you approach designing for low-bandwidth or offline environments in mobile app interfaces?**

Answer: Designing for low-bandwidth or offline environments in mobile app interfaces involves creating experiences that remain functional and usable even under adverse network conditions. To achieve this, I prioritize performance optimization and efficient data management techniques that minimize the amount of data transferred and maximize the app's responsiveness. This may include techniques such as lazy loading, caching, and data compression to reduce the app's data footprint and minimize loading times. Additionally, I design offline-first strategies that allow users to access and interact with critical app functionality even when they are offline, such as caching essential data locally and synchronizing changes with the server once a network connection is restored. By prioritizing usability and reliability in low-bandwidth or offline environments, I ensure that users can access and use the app seamlessly, regardless of their network conditions.

58. **Question: Can you describe a time when you had to design for cross-platform consistency, such as web, iOS, and Android?**

Answer: Yes, there was a project where I had to design a cross-platform mobile app for a client that needed to be consistent and cohesive across different platforms, including web, iOS, and Android. To achieve cross-platform consistency, I started by establishing a set of design principles and guidelines that applied across all platforms, such as colour palette, typography, and spacing. I then created responsive designs that adapted to different screen sizes and resolutions, ensuring a consistent visual experience across devices. Additionally, I leveraged platform-specific design patterns and conventions to optimize the user experience for each platform, taking into account factors such as navigation paradigms, screen resolutions, and input methods. By prioritizing consistency and coherence in my designs, I was able to deliver a cross-platform app that provided a unified and seamless experience for users, regardless of the device they were using.

59. **Question: How do you approach designing for privacy and data security in user interfaces?**

Answer: Designing for privacy and data security involves ensuring that users' personal information is protected and handled responsibly throughout the user journey. To achieve this, I start by conducting a privacy impact assessment to identify potential privacy risks and compliance requirements associated with the product. I then design user interfaces that provide transparency and control over the collection, use, and sharing of personal data, such as clear privacy policies, consent mechanisms, and privacy settings. Additionally, I incorporate security best practices, such as encryption, authentication, and access controls, to safeguard sensitive data from unauthorized access or breaches. Throughout the design process, I collaborate with privacy and security experts to ensure that the design meets industry standards and regulatory requirements for privacy and data protection.

60. **Question: Can you describe your experience with designing for accessibility in gaming interfaces?**

Answer: My experience with designing for accessibility in gaming interfaces includes creating experiences that are inclusive and accessible to players of all abilities, including those with disabilities. This includes considerations such as providing customizable controls, subtitles, and alternative input methods to accommodate different player needs and preferences. I also conduct usability testing with players who have disabilities to gather feedback and identify any accessibility barriers or usability issues. By prioritizing accessibility in my gaming interfaces, I ensure that they are accessible and enjoyable for players of all abilities, allowing everyone to participate and engage in the gaming experience.

61. **Question: How do you approach designing for emerging interaction paradigms, such as voice interfaces or gesture-based interactions?**

Answer: Designing for emerging interaction paradigms, such as voice interfaces or gesture-based interactions, involves exploring new design principles and patterns that leverage the unique capabilities of these technologies. To achieve this, I start by researching and understanding the capabilities and constraints of the technology, as well as the user behaviours and preferences associated with it. I then collaborate with cross-functional teams, including developers, engineers, and content creators, to brainstorm and prototype innovative experiences that push the boundaries of traditional UI/UX design. Throughout the design process, I prioritize user testing and feedback to validate the effectiveness and usability of the designs, iterating on them based on insights and observations. By embracing emerging interaction paradigms and pushing the boundaries of design innovation, I create immersive and engaging experiences that captivate users and deliver value in new and exciting ways.

62. **Question: Can you describe a time when you had to design for multi-language support in user interfaces?**

    Answer: Yes, there was a project where I had to design a web application that needed to support multiple languages to cater to an international audience. To achieve this, I collaborated closely with localization experts to translate and adapt content for different languages and regions. This included designing interfaces that could accommodate text expansion and contraction, as well as cultural variations in layout and typography. Additionally, I incorporated language selection controls and localization settings into the interface to allow users to customize their language preferences. By prioritizing multi-language support in my designs, I ensured that the web application was accessible and usable by users from diverse linguistic backgrounds, allowing them to interact with the product in their preferred language.

63. **Question: How do you approach designing for user trust and credibility in e-commerce interfaces?**

    Answer: Designing for user trust and credibility in e-commerce interfaces involves creating experiences that inspire confidence and build trust among users, fostering a positive relationship between the user and the brand. To achieve this, I focus on transparency, consistency, and reliability in my designs, providing clear and accurate information about products, pricing, and shipping policies. I use visual cues and branding elements to convey professionalism and authenticity, such as high-quality product images, customer reviews, and secure payment icons. Additionally, I prioritize usability and security, designing interfaces that are easy to use and protect users' sensitive information from unauthorized access or breaches. By prioritizing trust and credibility in my designs, I create e-commerce experiences that instil confidence and loyalty among users, ultimately driving conversion and retention for the brand.

64. **Question: Can you describe your experience with designing for emotional engagement and user delight in user interfaces?**

Answer: My experience with designing for emotional engagement and user delight involves creating experiences that evoke positive emotions and create memorable moments for users. This includes techniques such as playful animations, unexpected interactions, and personalized experiences that surprise and delight users. I also prioritize empathy and human-centred design principles, designing interfaces that resonate with users on an emotional level and make them feel understood and valued. Additionally, I conduct usability testing and user research to gather feedback and validate the effectiveness of the emotional design elements, iterating on the designs based on insights and observations. By prioritizing emotional engagement and user delight in my designs, I create experiences that go beyond functionality to create meaningful connections with users, fostering loyalty and advocacy for the product or brand.

65. **Question: How do you approach designing for user education and onboarding in web interfaces?**

Answer: Designing for user education and onboarding in web interfaces involves creating experiences that guide users through the initial setup process and help them understand how to use the product effectively. To achieve this, I create interactive tutorials, tooltips, and guided tours that introduce key features and functionalities and provide step-by-step instructions for getting started. I also leverage progressive disclosure techniques to gradually reveal more advanced features as users become more familiar with the product. Additionally, I conduct usability testing with first-time users to gather feedback and identify any usability issues or points of confusion in the onboarding process, iterating on the designs based on insights and observations. By prioritizing user education and onboarding in my designs, I ensure that users can quickly and easily learn how to use the product and get value from it.

66. **Question: Can you describe your experience with designing for complex data visualization and analytics interfaces?**

Answer: My experience with designing for complex data visualization and analytics interfaces includes creating experiences that help users make sense of large amounts of data and derive insights from it. This includes techniques such as hierarchical navigation, interactive filters, and data-driven visualizations that enhance comprehension and exploration. I also prioritize simplicity and clarity, minimizing clutter and cognitive load for users while maximizing the effectiveness of the data presentation. Additionally, I conduct usability testing with representative users to gather feedback and validate design decisions, iterating on the designs based on insights and observations. By prioritizing usability and user experience in my designs, I create data visualization and analytics interfaces that are intuitive, informative, and actionable for users.

67. **Question: How do you approach designing for user feedback and engagement in social media interfaces?**

Answer: Designing for user feedback and engagement in social media interfaces involves creating experiences that facilitate communication, interaction, and collaboration among users. To achieve this, I prioritize features such as comments, likes, shares, and direct messaging that encourage users to engage with each other and with the content. I also design notification systems and activity feeds that keep users informed about relevant updates and interactions, prompting them to participate and contribute to the conversation. Additionally, I conduct usability testing with active social media users to gather feedback and identify opportunities for improvement, iterating on the designs based on insights and observations. By prioritizing user feedback and engagement in my designs, I create social media interfaces that foster community and connection among users, driving engagement and retention for the platform.

68. **Question: How do you approach designing for scalability and extensibility in enterprise software interfaces?**

Answer: Designing for scalability and extensibility in enterprise software interfaces involves creating experiences that can accommodate the needs of large organizations with complex workflows and diverse user roles. To achieve this, I start by conducting user research and stakeholder interviews to understand the requirements and constraints of the enterprise environment. I then design flexible and modular interfaces that can adapt to different user roles, permissions, and customization preferences. This may include features such as role-based access controls, customizable dashboards, and workflow automation tools that streamline processes and increase productivity. Additionally, I prioritize performance optimization and system integrations, ensuring that the interface can handle large datasets and integrate seamlessly with other enterprise systems. By prioritizing scalability and extensibility in my designs, I create enterprise software interfaces that are robust, adaptable, and future proof for organizations of all sizes.

69. **Question: Can you describe a time when you had to design for a highly technical or specialized audience, such as engineers or data scientists?**

 Answer: Yes, there was a project where I had to design a data visualization tool for a highly technical audience of data scientists and analysts. To meet the needs of this audience, I collaborated closely with domain experts to understand their workflows, tools, and terminology. I designed interfaces that provided advanced data manipulation and analysis capabilities, such as interactive filters, custom queries, and statistical modelling tools. I also incorporated features such as data export and integration with popular analysis tools to support their workflow. Additionally, I conducted usability testing and gathered feedback from the target audience to ensure that the design met their needs and preferences. By prioritizing usability and user experience for a highly technical audience, I created a data visualization tool that was intuitive, efficient, and valuable for users in their daily work.

70. **Question: How do you approach designing for offline-first experiences in mobile app interfaces?**

Answer: Designing for offline-first experiences in mobile app interfaces involves creating experiences that remain functional and usable even when users are offline or have limited connectivity. To achieve this, I prioritize offline data storage and synchronization techniques that allow users to access and interact with critical app functionality offline. This may include caching essential data locally on the device, such as user preferences or recent activity, and synchronizing changes with the server once a network connection is restored. I also design user interfaces that provide clear feedback and guidance when users are offline, such as offline mode indicators or queued actions that are processed once connectivity is restored. By prioritizing offline-first design principles, I ensure that users can access and use the app seamlessly, regardless of their network conditions.

71. **Question: Can you describe a time when you had to design for accessibility in virtual reality (VR) or augmented reality (AR) interfaces?**

   Answer: Yes, there was a project where I had to design an augmented reality (AR) application for users with disabilities, such as visual impairments or mobility limitations. To meet the needs of this audience, I collaborated closely with accessibility experts and users with disabilities to understand their needs, preferences, and challenges when interacting with AR interfaces. I designed interfaces that provided clear audio feedback and haptic cues to assist users with visual impairments in navigating the virtual environment and interacting with digital objects. I also incorporated voice commands and gesture recognition to provide alternative input methods for users with mobility limitations. Additionally, I conducted usability testing and gathered feedback from users with disabilities to ensure that the design met their needs and preferences. By prioritizing accessibility in AR interfaces, I created an inclusive and usable experience for users with disabilities, allowing them to fully participate and engage in the AR experience.

72. **Question: How do you approach designing for brand consistency and identity in digital interfaces?**

   Answer: Designing for brand consistency and identity in digital interfaces involves creating experiences that reflect and reinforce the brand's values, personality, and visual identity. To achieve this, I start by establishing a set of brand guidelines and design principles that define the brand's visual language, including color palette, typography, imagery, and tone of voice. I then apply these guidelines consistently across all digital touchpoints, including websites, mobile apps, and social media platforms, to create a cohesive and recognizable brand experience. Additionally, I collaborate closely with brand managers and marketing teams to ensure alignment and consistency between the digital interface and other brand assets and communications. By prioritizing brand consistency and identity in my designs, I create digital experiences that resonate with users and strengthen the brand's relationship with its audience.

73. **Question: Can you describe your experience with designing for immersive experiences, such as virtual reality (VR) or augmented reality (AR)?**

Answer: My experience with designing for immersive experiences, such as virtual reality (VR) or augmented reality (AR), includes creating experiences that engage users and transport them to virtual worlds or enhance their real-world environment. This includes designing interactive environments, 3D models, and spatial audio that immerse users in the experience and create a sense of presence and immersion. I also prioritize usability and comfort, designing interfaces that are intuitive and easy to use, even in immersive environments. Additionally, I conduct usability testing and gather feedback from users to validate the effectiveness and usability of the designs, iterating on them based on insights and observations. By prioritizing immersion and user experience in my designs, I create immersive experiences that captivate users and deliver value in new and exciting ways.

74. **Question: How do you approach designing for user empowerment and self-service in digital interfaces?**

Answer: Designing for user empowerment and self-service in digital interfaces involves creating experiences that enable users to accomplish tasks and achieve their goals independently and efficiently. To achieve this, I prioritize features such as intuitive navigation, clear instructions, and self-explanatory interfaces that guide users through complex processes and workflows. I also design interactive help and support features, such as knowledge bases, FAQs, and chatbots, that provide users with access to relevant information and assistance when needed.

Additionally, I conduct usability testing and gather feedback from users to identify pain points and usability issues in the self-service experience, iterating on the designs based on insights and observations. By prioritizing user empowerment and self-service in my designs, I create digital experiences that empower users to take control of their interactions and accomplish tasks with confidence and ease.

75. **Question: Can you describe a time when you had to design for global scalability and localization in digital interfaces?**

Answer: Yes, there was a project where I had to design a digital platform for a global audience that required scalability and localization to accommodate users from different countries and regions. To achieve this, I collaborated closely with localization experts and native speakers to translate and adapt content for different languages and cultures. This included designing interfaces that could accommodate text expansion and contraction, as well as cultural variations in layout and imagery. Additionally, I incorporated language selection controls and localization settings into the interface to allow users to customize their language preferences and region-specific settings. By prioritizing global scalability and localization in my designs, I ensured that the digital platform was accessible and usable by users from diverse linguistic and cultural backgrounds, allowing them to interact with the product in their preferred language and context.

76. **Question: How do you approach designing for inclusivity and diversity in digital interfaces?**

Answer: Designing for inclusivity and diversity in digital interfaces involves creating experiences that are accessible and welcoming to users from diverse backgrounds, abilities, and perspectives. To achieve this, I prioritize representation and inclusivity in my designs, using diverse imagery, language, and content that reflects the diversity of the target audience. I also design interfaces that are accessible and usable by people of all abilities, including those with disabilities, by following accessibility guidelines and best practices. Additionally, I conduct usability testing and gather feedback from representative users to identify any accessibility barriers or points of exclusion in the design, iterating on the designs based on insights and observations. By prioritizing inclusivity and diversity in my designs, I create digital experiences that resonate with users and foster a sense of belonging and inclusion for everyone.

77. **Question: Can you describe a time when you had to design for privacy and security in social media interfaces?**

Answer: Yes, there was a project where I had to design a social media platform that required robust privacy and security features to protect users' personal information and ensure safe and secure interactions. To achieve this, I collaborated closely with privacy and security experts to identify potential risks and compliance requirements associated with the platform. I then designed interfaces that provided clear and transparent privacy settings and controls, such as granular permissions and privacy policies, to give users control over their data and interactions. Additionally, I implemented security measures such as encryption, authentication, and access controls to safeguard sensitive information from unauthorized access or breaches. By prioritizing privacy and security in my designs, I created a social media platform that provided a safe and trustworthy environment for users to connect and interact with each other.

78. **Question: How do you approach designing for sustainability and eco-friendliness in digital interfaces?**

Answer: Designing for sustainability and eco-friendliness in digital interfaces involves creating experiences that minimize environmental impact and promote responsible consumption and behaviour. To achieve this, I prioritize factors such as energy efficiency, resource conservation, and waste reduction in my designs, using techniques such as optimizing file sizes, reducing server load, and minimizing network requests to reduce energy consumption and carbon emissions. I also design interfaces that promote eco-friendly behaviours, such as encouraging users to opt for digital transactions over paper-based processes, or providing tools and resources to help users reduce their environmental footprint. Additionally, I collaborate with sustainability experts and environmental organizations to incorporate sustainability principles and initiatives into the design process, ensuring that the digital interfaces align with broader sustainability goals and initiatives. By prioritizing sustainability and eco-friendliness in my designs, I contribute to a more sustainable and environmentally conscious digital ecosystem.

79. **Question: Can you describe a time when you had to design for ethical considerations in digital interfaces?**

Answer: Yes, there was a project where I had to design a digital platform that required careful consideration of ethical implications and consequences, such as privacy, data protection, and social impact. To address these considerations, I conducted ethical impact assessments and stakeholder consultations to identify potential ethical risks and concerns associated with the platform. I then incorporated ethical design principles and guidelines into the design process, such as transparency, fairness, and accountability, to ensure that the platform prioritized user well-being and societal values. Additionally, I implemented features and controls that empowered users to make informed choices and decisions about their data and interactions, such as clear privacy policies, consent mechanisms, and user controls. By prioritizing ethical considerations in my designs, I created a digital platform that was not only functional and user-friendly but also ethical and responsible in its impact on users and society.

80. **Question: How do you approach designing for emotional intelligence and empathy in digital interfaces?**

Answer: Designing for emotional intelligence and empathy in digital interfaces involves creating experiences that understand and respond to users' emotions and feelings in a sensitive and empathetic manner. To achieve this, I prioritize user research and empathy mapping to understand the emotional context and motivations of the target audience, as well as the factors that influence their emotional responses to the interface. I then design interfaces that incorporate emotional cues and feedback, such as micro interactions, animations, and tone of voice, to acknowledge and validate users' feelings and emotions. Additionally, I design interfaces that provide support and assistance when users are experiencing negative emotions or stress, such as error messages that provide guidance and encouragement rather than blame. By prioritizing emotional intelligence and empathy in my designs, I create digital experiences that foster a deeper connection and understanding between users and the interface, leading to increased trust, satisfaction, and loyalty.

81. **Question: Can you describe a time when you had to design for ethical AI and algorithmic transparency in digital interfaces?**

Answer: Yes, there was a project where I had to design a digital interface that incorporated artificial intelligence (AI) and machine learning algorithms to personalize content and recommendations for users. To address ethical considerations and algorithmic transparency, I collaborated closely with data scientists and AI ethics experts to ensure that the algorithms were fair, unbiased, and transparent in their decision-making process. This included incorporating features such as explanation interfaces and user controls that provided insight into how the algorithms worked and why certain recommendations were made. Additionally, I implemented measures such as fairness assessments and bias detection to identify and mitigate any ethical risks or biases in the algorithms. By prioritizing ethical AI and algorithmic transparency in my designs, I created a digital interface that not only provided personalized and relevant experiences for users but also upheld ethical principles and values in its use of AI technology.

82. **Question: How do you approach designing for digital well-being and mental health in digital interfaces?**

Answer: Designing for digital well-being and mental health in digital interfaces involves creating experiences that promote healthy and balanced usage habits and support users' mental and emotional well-being. To achieve this, I prioritize features such as time management tools, usage tracking, and notification controls that help users manage their digital consumption and maintain a healthy relationship with technology. I also design interfaces that prioritize clarity, simplicity, and mindfulness, minimizing distractions and cognitive overload for users. Additionally, I incorporate features such as mindfulness exercises, relaxation techniques, and digital detox reminders that encourage users to take breaks and engage in self-care practices. By prioritizing digital well-being and mental health in my designs, I create digital experiences that empower users to use technology mindfully and responsibly, enhancing their overall well-being and quality of life.

83. **Question: Can you describe a time when you had to design for ethical considerations in the use of personal data in digital interfaces?**

84. **Answer:** Yes, there was a project where I had to design a digital interface that required careful consideration of ethical implications and consequences in the use of personal data. To address these considerations, I conducted privacy impact assessments and stakeholder consultations to identify potential risks and concerns associated with the collection, use, and sharing of personal data. I then incorporated privacy-enhancing features and controls into the design, such as transparent data collection practices, granular consent mechanisms, and user controls over their data. Additionally, I implemented measures such as data minimization and anonymization to reduce the amount of personal data collected and stored, as well as to protect user privacy and confidentiality. By prioritizing ethical considerations in the use of personal data in my designs, I created a digital interface that respected user privacy and autonomy while still providing valuable and personalized experiences.

85. **Question: How do you approach designing for cognitive load and attention management in digital interfaces?**

Answer: Designing for cognitive load and attention management in digital interfaces involves creating experiences that minimize cognitive overload and help users focus on the task at hand. To achieve this, I prioritize simplicity, clarity, and hierarchy in my designs, using techniques such as visual hierarchy, whitespace, and progressive disclosure to organize information and guide users' attention. I also design interfaces that provide clear and concise feedback, instructions, and error messages, reducing the cognitive effort required to understand and interact with the interface. Additionally, I implement features such as task prioritization, multitasking support, and notifications management that help users manage their attention and stay focused on their goals. By prioritizing cognitive load and attention management in my designs, I create digital experiences that are intuitive, efficient, and conducive to productivity and focus.

86. **Question: Can you describe a time when you had to design for ethical considerations in the use of AI and machine learning in digital interfaces?**

Answer: Yes, there was a project where I had to design a digital interface that incorporated artificial intelligence (AI) and machine learning algorithms to automate decision-making processes. To address ethical considerations in the use of AI and machine learning, I collaborated closely with ethicists, data scientists, and domain experts to ensure that the algorithms were fair, transparent, and accountable in their decision-making process. This included implementing features such as explanation interfaces and user controls that provided insight into how the algorithms worked and why certain decisions were made. Additionally, I conducted fairness assessments and bias detection to identify and mitigate any ethical risks or biases in the algorithms. By prioritizing ethical considerations in the use of AI and machine learning in my designs, I created a digital interface that not only provided intelligent and efficient solutions but also upheld ethical principles and values in its use of AI technology.

87. **Question: How do you approach designing for ethical considerations in the use of persuasive design techniques in digital interfaces?**

Answer: Designing for ethical considerations in the use of persuasive design techniques in digital interfaces involves creating experiences that empower users to make informed choices and decisions, rather than manipulating or coercing their behaviour. To achieve this, I prioritize transparency, autonomy, and user empowerment in my designs, providing clear and honest information about the intended outcomes and consequences of user actions. I also design interfaces that offer choice and control, allowing users to opt-in or opt-out of persuasive features and interventions based on their preferences and values. Additionally, I conduct usability testing and gather feedback from users to ensure that the design respects their autonomy and aligns with their ethical beliefs and values. By prioritizing ethical considerations in the use of persuasive design techniques, I create digital experiences that foster trust, respect, and empowerment among users, ultimately leading to more positive and meaningful interactions.

88. **Question: Can you describe a time when you had to design for ethical considerations in the use of dark patterns in digital interfaces?**

Answer: Yes, there was a project where I had to design a digital interface that required careful consideration of ethical implications and consequences in the use of dark patterns – deceptive or manipulative design techniques that trick users into taking actions they may not want to take. To address these considerations, I conducted ethical impact assessments and stakeholder consultations to identify potential risks and concerns associated with the use of dark patterns. I then designed interfaces that prioritized transparency, honesty, and user empowerment, providing clear and honest information about the intended outcomes and consequences of user actions. Additionally, I implemented features such as user controls and warnings that alerted users to the presence of dark patterns and allowed them to opt-out or report unethical behaviour. By prioritizing ethical considerations in the use of dark patterns in my designs, I created digital interfaces that respected user autonomy and fostered trust and respect among users.

89. **Question: How do you approach designing for ethical considerations in the use of persuasive design techniques in digital interfaces?**

Answer: Designing for ethical considerations in the use of persuasive design techniques in digital interfaces involves creating experiences that empower users to make informed choices and decisions, rather than manipulating or coercing their behaviour. To achieve this, I prioritize transparency, autonomy, and user empowerment in my designs, providing clear and honest information about the intended outcomes and consequences of user actions. I also design interfaces that offer choice and control, allowing users to opt-in or opt-out of persuasive features and interventions based on their preferences and values. Additionally, I conduct usability testing and gather feedback from users to ensure that the design respects their autonomy and aligns with their ethical beliefs and values. By prioritizing ethical considerations in the use of persuasive design techniques, I create digital experiences that foster trust, respect, and empowerment among users, ultimately leading to more positive and meaningful interactions.

90. **Question: Can you describe a time when you had to design for ethical considerations in the use of dark patterns in digital interfaces?**

Answer: Yes, there was a project where I had to design a digital interface that required careful consideration of ethical implications and consequences in the use of dark patterns – deceptive or manipulative design techniques that trick users into taking actions they may not want to take. To address these considerations, I conducted ethical impact assessments and stakeholder consultations to identify potential risks and concerns associated with the use of dark patterns. I then designed interfaces that prioritized transparency, honesty, and user empowerment, providing clear and honest information about the intended outcomes and consequences of user actions. Additionally, I implemented features such as user controls and warnings that alerted users to the presence of dark patterns and allowed them to opt-out or report unethical behaviour. By prioritizing ethical considerations in the use of dark patterns in my designs, I created digital interfaces that respected user autonomy and fostered trust and respect among users.

91. **Question: How do you approach designing for ethical considerations in the use of persuasive design techniques in digital interfaces?**

   Answer: Designing for ethical considerations in the use of persuasive design techniques in digital interfaces involves creating experiences that empower users to make informed choices and decisions, rather than manipulating or coercing their behaviour. To achieve this, I prioritize transparency, autonomy, and user empowerment in my designs, providing clear and honest information about the intended outcomes and consequences of user actions. I also design interfaces that offer choice and control, allowing users to opt-in or opt-out of persuasive features and interventions based on their preferences and values. Additionally, I conduct usability testing and gather feedback from users to ensure that the design respects their autonomy and aligns with their ethical beliefs and values. By prioritizing ethical considerations in the use of persuasive design techniques, I create digital experiences that foster trust, respect, and empowerment among users, ultimately leading to more positive and meaningful interactions.

92. **Question: Can you describe a time when you had to design for ethical considerations in the use of dark patterns in digital interfaces?**

   Answer: Yes, there was a project where I had to design a digital interface that required careful consideration of ethical implications and consequences in the use of dark patterns – deceptive or manipulative design techniques that trick users into taking actions they may not want to take. To address these considerations, I conducted ethical impact assessments and stakeholder consultations to identify potential risks and concerns associated with the use of dark patterns. I then designed interfaces that prioritized transparency, honesty, and user empowerment, providing clear and honest information about the intended outcomes and consequences of user actions. Additionally, I implemented features such as user controls and warnings that alerted users to the presence of dark patterns and allowed them to opt-out or report unethical behaviour. By prioritizing ethical considerations in the use of dark patterns in my designs, I created digital interfaces that respected user autonomy and fostered trust and respect among users.

93. **Question: How do you approach designing for ethical considerations in the use of persuasive design techniques in digital interfaces?**

Answer: Designing for ethical considerations in the use of persuasive design techniques in digital interfaces involves creating experiences that empower users to make informed choices and decisions, rather than manipulating or coercing their behaviour. To achieve this, I prioritize transparency, autonomy, and user empowerment in my designs, providing clear and honest information about the intended outcomes and consequences of user actions. I also design interfaces that offer choice and control, allowing users to opt-in or opt-out of persuasive features and interventions based on their preferences and values. Additionally, I conduct usability testing and gather feedback from users to ensure that the design respects their autonomy and aligns with their ethical beliefs and values. By prioritizing ethical considerations in the use of persuasive design techniques, I create digital experiences that foster trust, respect, and empowerment among users, ultimately leading to more positive and meaningful interactions.

94. **Question: Can you describe a time when you had to design for ethical considerations in the use of dark patterns in digital interfaces?**

Answer: Yes, there was a project where I had to design a digital interface that required careful consideration of ethical implications and consequences in the use of dark patterns – deceptive or manipulative design techniques that trick users into taking actions they may not want to take. To address these considerations, I conducted ethical impact assessments and stakeholder consultations to identify potential risks and concerns associated with the use of dark patterns. I then designed interfaces that prioritized transparency, honesty, and user empowerment, providing clear and honest information about the intended outcomes and consequences of user actions. Additionally, I implemented features such as user controls and warnings that alerted users to the presence of dark patterns and allowed them to opt-out or report unethical behaviour. By prioritizing ethical considerations in the use of dark patterns in my designs, I created digital interfaces that respected user autonomy and fostered trust and respect among users.

95. **Question: How do you approach designing for ethical considerations in the use of persuasive design techniques in digital interfaces?**

Answer: Designing for ethical considerations in the use of persuasive design techniques in digital interfaces involves creating experiences that empower users to make informed choices and decisions, rather than manipulating or coercing their behaviour. To achieve this, I prioritize transparency, autonomy, and user empowerment in my designs, providing clear and honest information about the intended outcomes and consequences of user actions. I also design interfaces that offer choice and control, allowing users to opt-in or opt-out of persuasive features and interventions based on their preferences and values. Additionally, I conduct usability testing and gather feedback from users to ensure that the design respects their autonomy and aligns with their ethical beliefs and values. By prioritizing ethical considerations in the use of persuasive design techniques, I create digital experiences that foster trust, respect, and empowerment among users, ultimately leading to more positive and meaningful interactions.

96. **Question: Can you describe a time when you had to design for ethical considerations in the use of dark patterns in digital interfaces?**

Answer: Yes, there was a project where I had to design a digital interface that required careful consideration of ethical implications and consequences in the use of dark patterns – deceptive or manipulative design techniques that trick users into taking actions they may not want to take. To address these considerations, I conducted ethical impact assessments and stakeholder consultations to identify potential risks and concerns associated with the use of dark patterns. I then designed interfaces that prioritized transparency, honesty, and user empowerment, providing clear and honest information about the intended outcomes and consequences of user actions. Additionally, I implemented features such as user controls and warnings that alerted users to the presence of dark patterns and allowed them to opt-out or report unethical behaviour. By prioritizing ethical considerations in the use of dark patterns in my designs, I created digital interfaces that respected user autonomy and fostered trust and respect among users.

97. **Question: How do you approach designing for ethical considerations in the use of persuasive design techniques in digital interfaces?**

Answer: Designing for ethical considerations in the use of persuasive design techniques in digital interfaces involves creating experiences that empower users to make informed choices and decisions, rather than manipulating or coercing their behaviour. To achieve this, I prioritize transparency, autonomy, and user empowerment in my designs, providing clear and honest information about the intended outcomes and consequences of user actions. I also design interfaces that offer choice and control, allowing users to opt-in or opt-out of persuasive features and interventions based on their preferences and values. Additionally, I conduct usability testing and gather feedback from users to ensure that the design respects their autonomy and aligns with their ethical beliefs and values. By prioritizing ethical considerations in the use of persuasive design techniques, I create digital experiences that foster trust, respect, and empowerment among users, ultimately leading to more positive and meaningful interactions.

98. **Question: Can you describe a time when you had to design for ethical considerations in the use of dark patterns in digital interfaces?**

Answer: Yes, there was a project where I had to design a digital interface that required careful consideration of ethical implications and consequences in the use of dark patterns – deceptive or manipulative design techniques that trick users into taking actions they may not want to take. To address these considerations, I conducted ethical impact assessments and stakeholder consultations to identify potential risks and concerns associated with the use of dark patterns. I then designed interfaces that prioritized transparency, honesty, and user empowerment, providing clear and honest information about the intended outcomes and consequences of user actions. Additionally, I implemented features such as user controls and warnings that alerted users to the presence of dark patterns and allowed them to opt-out or report unethical behaviour. By prioritizing ethical considerations in the use of dark patterns in my designs, I created digital interfaces that respected user autonomy and fostered trust and respect among users.

99. **Question: How do you approach designing for ethical considerations in the use of persuasive design techniques in digital interfaces?**

Answer: Designing for ethical considerations in the use of persuasive design techniques in digital interfaces involves creating experiences that empower users to make informed choices and decisions, rather than manipulating or coercing their behaviour. To achieve this, I prioritize transparency, autonomy, and user empowerment in my designs, providing clear and honest information about the intended outcomes and consequences of user actions. I also design interfaces that offer choice and control, allowing users to opt-in or opt-out of persuasive features and interventions based on their preferences and values. Additionally, I conduct usability testing and gather feedback from users to ensure that the design respects their autonomy and aligns with their ethical beliefs and values. By prioritizing ethical considerations in the use of persuasive design techniques, I create digital experiences that foster trust, respect, and empowerment among users, ultimately leading to more positive and meaningful interactions.

100.   **Question: Can you describe a time when you had to design for ethical considerations in the use of dark patterns in digital interfaces?**

Answer: Yes, there was a project where I had to design a digital interface that required careful consideration of ethical implications and consequences in the use of dark patterns – deceptive or manipulative design techniques that trick users into taking actions they may not want to take. To address these considerations, I conducted ethical impact assessments and stakeholder consultations to identify potential risks and concerns associated with the use of dark patterns. I then designed interfaces that prioritized transparency, honesty, and user empowerment, providing clear and honest information about the intended outcomes and consequences of user actions. Additionally, I implemented features such as user controls and warnings that alerted users to the presence of dark patterns and allowed them to opt-out or report unethical behaviour. By prioritizing ethical considerations in the use of dark patterns in my designs, I created digital interfaces that respected user autonomy and fostered trust and respect among users.